Become A Powerful Creator

Realize Your Purpose

LER'E "HUSTLE GOD" GARRETT

Become A Powerful Creator

DEDICATION

To My Children Niles Seawood V, Kaleel Garrett
And The People I love.

*"We all have the power to bring our dreams into
reality, and that's why it is your purpose to
Become A Powerful Creator"* **~Hustle God**

CONTENTS

ACKNOWLEDGMENTS

First and foremost The Most High, my children Niles and Kaleel, my father may he rest in peace, my grandfather Samuel Jourdon, my aunt Tiola, my sister Samantha, Publishing Advantage Group, Deonna, my educators, my community and life.

INTRODUCTION

One of the greatest struggles we as humans face is finding our purpose in life. The inability to discover one's purpose can lead to feelings of hopelessness. Hope is what allows one the ability to construct a fulfilling and satisfying life. It is hope combined with an attitude of expectation and optimism that one has which allows an individual to receive the things that the heart desires. Ones hope to realize their purpose for existing is based on that individual's personal life experience along with the belief that life itself is meaningful. This is why hopelessness can be detrimental, even paralyzing to the human beings conscious evolution. Without hope, one loses the will that is necessary to create a meaningful life. Our souls yearn for more than we experience in the lives we live, yet we hunger for those experiences even though we do not quite understand what is required to fulfill this desire. Many often suffer from disturbing, recurring, intrusive, invasive visions and versions of themselves, living a life that individual desires but has not acquired and feels it may be farfetched and impossible to attain. The visions don't align with the self the visionary is familiar with or in other words the imagined self doesn't aligned with the known self or real self. The ego is manifested out of doubt, leading to the prevention of self-actualization which occurs when one's visions of self, or ideal self, aligns with the known self or "real self."

Becoming a powerful creator requires the ability to self- actualize one's identity for the purpose of merging two seemingly separate worlds into one. As a child, I, like many others growing up in the "ghetto" had limited exposure to the so called "real world," instead, there existed an "ideal world," a microcosm that lacked congruency in culture, beliefs and systemic architecture to the macrocosm. Even still, I was constantly plagued with visions of me in another life, one I had never seen or experienced before, yet I felt strongly connected to its reality and the feeling that it was for me. Like most children, I was unaware that there were limitations to fulfilling my dreams and allowed my real self to begin taking steps to line up with my future self. Being in the mind of a child, I was completely unaware that these worlds were separated by an invisible class system. I believed that all one needed to live their dreams was to do the work required to create one's vision. Unbeknownst to me, there must be a series of synchronicities that occur in one's life that allows for the necessary alignments of positioning and purpose. In other words, it is not just what you do, it's also how, when, where and why it's done, that aligns you to your purpose. Position always references the intersection of two points, meaning that it's the meeting of two or more of these postulates occurs for positioning oneself to their purpose.

Every living thing was uniquely created from the inception of life as we know it. The maturation of a caterpillar to a butterfly is like no other practice of transformation and self-actualization one can witness on earth. The caterpillar knows its reason for existence. It lives to become a butterfly. What more is a caterpillar than you that the Creator would not give you a reason for living, an objective, and an idea of what you are to become? Just as the caterpillar has the power to become a butterfly, you also can become a powerful creator. To become a powerful creator, one must first, realize their power and purpose. Since we were all created equally, that means we are all were born with the power to love ourselves, the power to govern ourselves and the power to manifest our hearts desires and to fulfill one's purpose, it is the greatest desire of the heart. One who has the intentions to manifest their hearts desires must first know what it is that the heart desires and focus intensely on producing that craving to satisfy the ultimate desire of one's heart.

One's purpose is uniquely tailored for that person at birth, it is like a fingerprint. No two people will have the exact same purpose in life. While there may be similarities in purposes of others, there are distinct differences that makes each exclusive to each conscious observer. These observations assist one in the process of realizing the purpose for that individual. Realizing one's purpose requires an introspective process of self-reflection, self- realization and self-awareness. These qualities assist an individual in the processes of discovering their purpose, aligning with their purpose, confirming their purpose, affirming their purpose and lastly manifesting and living out and in their purpose. To live a life of purpose is the highest form of accomplishment in our lives and those who wish to live with purpose must first become a powerful creator to create the atmosphere for their purpose to be produced.

The atmosphere required for one to shape their purpose is based on the alignment of five specific forces: consciousness, time, space, frequency and will. These are the five unseen qualities of the fourth dimension that need to align in a specific nature for a being to become a powerful creator. Limitations such as finance, mobility, formal education and other social constructs that become barriers in a third-dimension being's ability to manifest and these limitations can restrict progress towards one's purpose.

Consciousness has a significant role in one's ability to manifest their purpose. Consciousness can be loosely defined as your state of awareness, your state of being is recognized as an unseen place connecting to a physical time and awareness and is your ability to perceive this location minus its third dimensional representation. This is the necessary alignment with consciousness to time and space, that must occur for one to become a powerful creator, all of which exist in the physical reality as well as unseen forces. Another way to define consciousness is the dimensional state of vibrational frequency one's cellular structure resonates at.

There are twelve possible dimensional states

one can experience and resonate within. The ability to exist in multiple dimensions simultaneously is a concept known as multidimensionality. An example of this can be observed in one's ability to exist as a third dimensional being in fifth dimensional consciousness. As the consciousness of humanity reaches a critical mass point, many three- dimensional beings are swept into a fifth dimensional collective consciousness and will start to experience symptoms of multidimensionality. Third dimensional beings start to experience trials of clear and vivid visions almost like dreams. At this point, the awareness of self has deep emotional connects also known as empathy. One may have experiences of a voice in the inner voice, psychic experiences such as déjà vu, flashbacks, premonitions, strong intuition and sense of perception or awareness of self in altered dimensional states.

One being the lowest dimensional states of consciousness and its existence is the foundation of the physical form, including, minerals, water and genetic codes or DNA. Beings resonating with the first-dimension frequency lack depth and are unconscious of the five physical senses. It's the core awakening dimension that connects the being to the entire physical world on a molecular level. Although it is the lowest dimension a being can ascend to, it is also the gateway between the macrocosm and the microcosm or the seen and unseen things of the universe where the highest of the unseen things exist in the void of the twelfth dimension. The first dimension is the physical representation of the quantum world of protons, electrons and nuclei. Its dimension is ambiguous in that it could be considered both the first and the last dimension. Anything before the first dimension is a void and what exists after the void could be considered the first dimension in a third dimensional paradigm.

The second dimension is the dimensional state one ascends to after evolving from the first dimension, and consciousness begins to align with the physical being. Although at a low consciousness state, the cellular structures that modest increase in vibrational frequency from the first dimension is sufficient for one to become aware of space and time. This awareness creates a small amount of depth and perception in one's thinking. Awareness is concentrated towards the biological system which communicates to basic survival needs within the being. Basic survival needs are eating, drinking water, body temperature maintenance and proper responses to stimuli such as pain, light, gravity and touch. Although still unaware of the five physical senses, the nervous system acts to direct the body to perform basic life functions.

Two-dimensional life forms manifest in the physical third dimension, as the plant and animal kingdom, usually thought to be influenced by spiritual beings such as devas, fairies and dragons. Three-dimensional physical beings with two-dimensional consciousness would be considered imbeciles by the third dimensional beings, whom have ascended to an even higher vibrational state and exist in a three-dimensional conscious awareness and are capable of higher thought processes.

Higher thought processes occur in the third dimension because one's awareness to the physical world occurs through the five senses. The five senses allow the third dimensional beings to explore the world, thus creating experiences that become knowledge over time and wisdom with understanding. Our dense bodies are formed by the alignment of one's low vibrational consciousness with a specific space and time. This alignment of the physical being also aligns to the planetary conscious of the physical third dimensional world. Beings in this state of consciousness are aware of themselves and the existence of the universe. Higher thought processes lead to feelings of a sense of collective consciousness and the unknown answers to the unknown questions is what sends one on a quest to further exploration of life in this realm, ultimately leading to the necessary increase of vibrational frequency to ascend a being into a fourth- dimensional consciousness state.

Spatial depth in the fourth dimensional state allows for this state of conscious awareness. This awareness is achieved by the specific alignment of frequency required to raise the vibrational state of the cellular structure for the being to ascend to the higher dimensional state which is the place and time where the consciousness is manifested. Beings in this dimension become aware of the spirit and can acquire the ability to communicate with those entities through higher spiritual methods, such as meditation and use of the sixth sense also known as extra sensory perception. Extra sensory perception in the third dimensional being is known as intuition or clairvoyance in the fifth dimension. Extra sensory perception or ESP is exactly what it says - your senses have an increased or extra ability to perceive and interpret the environment. ESP allows one to begin to experience multiple paradigms, where in the third dimension the paradigms were linear and there were no intersections to allow for multiple potentials for outcomes of manifesting thought and thus, beings were limited to how they could manifest due to their limited perception of their environment.

The fourth-dimensional state is known as the gateway dimension. It serves as a grooming location for those destined to ascend to the fifth dimension and higher. It is in the fourth dimension that the near-death experience occurs. In preparation for ascension towards the higher dimensions, the ego developed through life experiences must die off and allow for the resurrection of one's soul to acquire fifth dimensional alignment. A person's will is developed during this process and is now working to align with one's consciousness, space, time and frequency to bring forth the enchanting experience of fifth-dimensional consciousness.

While in fifth-dimensional consciousness, the fourth- dimensional being is still being groomed for the evolution of a fifth-dimensional being. During this process, a universal conscious is developed, and one becomes aware of their personal power to create. As one progresses through the fourth dimension preparing for resurrection into the fifth dimension, the beings moral thought is developed. Thus, the understanding of concepts like right or wrong, heaven or hell and dark and light are perceived as far less polarizing in the realization that all things are created by the conscious observer to bring forth the being ordained to fulfill one's purpose. In the enchantment of this dimensional state, one is permitted to experience the magic of the spirit realms, conveyed by unseen entities such as gods, goddesses, and disembodied beings who work with your manifested higher-self to guide you towards your purpose for existence.

The expansion of the fifth dimension is due to its awareness of the soul or the awakening of the soul as consciousness, a microcosm of the macrocosm of the universal consciousness. Universal consciousness is the ability to experience oneness of all that is. At this point the once fragmented world begins to unite and coalesce into one unit. This unit could be compared to the body and you like a limb or an organ, you are a member of that body.

Once mindfulness of the whole body is achieved, one begins to heal and is thus allowed to move into the light body which is less massive yet more youthful and energetic than the preceding dense body. The result of this integration of dense body and light body results in the development of a stellar being, one which resonates in the frequency of unconditional love and becomes androgynous or genderless. This combination of traits helps one to reach and maintain Christ- consciousness by also abstaining from sexual activity a practice known as celibacy the being harnesses the energy necessary to will their desires into the physical reality.

The miraculous beings are reincarnated into the physical bodies of the ones whose consciousness has ascended to the fifth dimension thus creating a fifth-dimensional being who has walked through the valley of the shadow of death and has arrived at heaven's door. These beings now contain divine will and the awareness of their powerful ability to duplicate themselves in every dimension and project whichever self-chosen from whatever dimension one chooses to represent them in the dense physical dimensions.

As a stellar being with universal consciousness, one is cognizant of their ability to project their light bodies into the higher dimensions and thus access their Akashic records, which allows one access to understanding of communication in the third language. The third language is a means of communicating consciously as to convey symbols and conceptual thought into the first language for interpretation in the physical dimensions. The transference of conscious communication into a physical form of communication, allows for the one accessing the higher dimensions of consciousness to be more exciting, quick and astute with their responses to stimuli stemming from the physical dimensions.

The accessing of higher dimension through the fifth- dimensional light body is a concept known as soul- projecting where the physical portion of the stellar being remains in the physical dimensions, while the light body aspect of the stellar-being is projected consciously into the sixth- dimension and those beyond. In the sixth dimension, the light body can access the astrological genetic code. These astrological genetic codes are required to project one's consciousness into the seventh dimension. The seventh dimension is the launch dimension where from the soul projects to the higher dimensions, but first the blueprint, which is parallel to a road map, must be known to move from dimension to dimension. That is why the seventh dimension is known as the dimension of exploration since one is able to travel throughout the dimensional spectrum in the stellar body creating their own blueprint for creation. One travels back and forth through the dimensions to retrieve valuable information from the unseen dimensions and can then use the data to make clear high-quality decisions that yield the desired intent in the physical realm or what is known as the third dimension.

The movement throughout the dimensions in the stellar body is so fast that the physical world appears to stand still. In that moment, the loose connection to the dense physical world allows for the proper conscious expansion necessary to allow for the dimensional evolution to occur. Once the being has reached a state of dimensional evolution, the astral journey can begin. During the dimensional journey one is accompanied by members of their soul groups. A soul group is a group of individual souls which are the mates to the soul of the beings they are entangled with.

Each being has many soul mates. Soul mates are those who were created simultaneously with the souls of that group. Soul mates work as a group to accomplish alignments and synchronizations in the physical realm. Soul mates are manifested in the eighth dimension and are matched to beings in the physical dimension unbeknownst to the lower dimensional beings and this is why often in life we are at some time attracted to our soul mates. It's as if our hearts have chosen them, male or female, known or stranger, family or friend and even many miles away. The connection to your soul mates is like that of the attraction of magnets. To understand the concept of soulmates one should imagine that when one is sleeping, one is entering an altered state of consciousness, which allows for the access to the higher dimensions. During this exploration one communes with their soul mates as if to bathe in thyself. This communion leads to a familiarity, still experienced once one breaks from their sleep. Yet, to experience the attraction with cognizance, one must hear or see the soul of their soul mate in the physical to validate what was felt during the vision and this can be achieved because the eyes and the ears remembers all it has witnessed in all states of consciousness or existence on a subconscious level.

One could imagine a soul group as one's whole body and each member, its parts. These members come together to manifest as a new form or vehicle in another dimension. In the physical, these manifestations are three-dimensional beings have what is known as the corporeal body or the physical body. This physical body is a dense collection of members in one's soul group and soul are groups are able to manifest as many physical bodies as necessary to accomplish one's purpose. On the physical level, we use our hearts to discern who of the many physical beings belong to one's soul group. This discernment is a magnetic energy experienced by the heart, through electrical sensations, which are experienced as emotion through a process known as entanglements. Emotions are the universe's way of communicating with a conscious being. Those emotions are filtered through the brain to the heart through the bodies' neurological system to be deciphered as thoughts which can be acted upon by the conscious being.

The action one chooses is through one's freedom of choice, a choice to understand the emotions or to ignore them. Understanding of

one's emotions guides the conscious being towards
necessary alignments and synchronicities needed
to manifest one's desires in the physical, dense
third dimension. Manifestations in the third
dimension are accomplished by harmonious
cooperation between members of one's soul group.
The magnetic connection to members of one's soul
group creates a sense of familiarity with the other
being, causing an instant attraction to one another
which is magnetic.

Soul group members may choose to manifest
together as a group or individually. An example of
this from the eighth-dimension soul group realm to
the third-dimension physical dense realm as a
group, is a rainforest, the ocean, the sky or the
earth's crust. On the other hand, another example
of this soul group split during third dimensional
manifestation is an individual human being, the
elements, animals and or plants. The choice in type
of manifestation is relative to the purpose of the
soul group and may consist of varying entities
within the dimensions which can be embodied in
the third dimensional physical realm. An
illustration of this would be a soul group
containing and element such as fire, an animal,
such as a cat, a human being, such as a woman,

and a plant, such as cannabis in varying syndications. The members unites in the third dimension as a conglomerate to carry out alignments and synchronicities, which allows for the group to work toward its collective goal of manifesting the soul's' purpose.

The soul's purpose was chosen even before the soul group was formed in the eighth dimension, by a homogenized consciousness which exist in the ninth dimension as a stellar planetary body, a galaxy, a universe or a multidimensional consciousness. The ninth dimension is the formless transitional state, the dimension that exist between conception of thought and inception of thought to the manifestation of thought. The ninth dimension is the place where pure conscious thought decides to evolve from the formless to the formed and begins the process of evolution. One could akin this process to one who on the physical third dimensional realm, undergoes a drastic life change, the change would start with a thought of what is to be changed, and then with the inception of how to create such change, followed by the evolution needed to create change within that individual to then manifest into reality a change that was once just a thought.

Inorganic matter is used to create the vehicle required by the conscious being, inorganic matter is a compound that contains carbon, one of the building blocks of life, but is not a living thing. Inorganic substances used to evolve the vehicle of the conscious body can include in addition to carbon, cyanides, and other complexes mineral in nature. These compounds generate gravity which forms a tight magnetic connection between the substances that pulls them together in a hierarchical structure, chosen by its emanation of power, such as the comparison between the powers of the sky to a blade of grass. In this comparison, one could see how the sky has the power to hold together the constellations, while the grass has the power to protect and blanket parts of the earth under certain conditions, meanwhile the sky is always in the sky.

There is also a structure of hierarchical interdependence in the formation process of the evolved ninth dimensional being through 5D+ self-awareness, as exampled by people needing the earth or the earth needing the sun, all this work is carried out by the conscious thought of the multidimensional being and is part of the process of manifesting the soul's purpose. It is the state of transition from formless thought to evolution of physical form and the birth of manifestation from that which is merely subjective to that which is quite objective and purposeful. The formless thoughts are experienced by the 5D+ being for manifestation in the third dimension through the emotional body, which then transfers the data into its physical form at the cellular level. On a cellular level, complexes are formed which will direct the physical body and in turn direct the mental body, producing high conscious and aligned thoughts.

The consciousness that forms the formless universe of the ninth dimension, which is a transitional state between conception of thought and inception of thought exist in the tenth dimension the dimension of pure conscious thought. Pure conscious though from inception; has potential to manifest, is born, develops, matures and if it does not reach conception, dies and this is what is known as a cosmic day. In the physical third dimension, this can be likened to, a woman reaching full term pregnancy, giving birth, developing and maturing that child but if there is no purpose in the life of that child. The child is dead or stillborn.

The tenth dimension is the place within the

multidimensional structure where, nothing becomes something. The beginning of the formed conception from the end of the formless inception, the alpha or beginning of formed from the omega the end of the formless and is represented by the 1 and 0, which is the birth death cycle of the thoughts from the birth or on position of the formed, to the death or off position of the formless. The tenth dimension is place of the birth of consciousness before it forms into thought out of the void of the formless. In understanding this principal, one begins to understand the potential for many universes, seeing as the tenth dimension is a cosmic entity invariable within the universe. Thus, the potential for many universes is enumerable such is the outline of the void of the tenth dimension with the potential to produce infinite 3D universes with hard centers from pure conscious intention.

The pure conscious thought of the tenth dimension is manifested using the yin and yang forces of the universe to create the magnetic energy that holds the 3D universe together and gives it a solid core. The opposing forces of the universe start with the darkness creating the pure light or the Christ which opposes the darkness and attracts to one another and so on with the elements of fire and water. Then, the contracting and expanding of space to form matter. This process of development occurs on the quantum plane of existence and is unseen and at times unperceivable. This is where the energy, the matter, and the light join to become the unified conscious or Christ conscious needed to produce the light that will balance out the darkness of the void, for the formless to begin to hold form.

Awareness of the production of the Christ conscious activates the cosmic DNA and divine will is put into action to begin manifestation from pure conscious subjective thought to conscious objective thought. A 5D+ being through multidimensionality has the power to project the Christ conscious into their dense physical three-dimensional body. The Christ consciousness is the DNA data download that directs one's will toward the truth and leads to an even greater connection to the light within, which builds the 5D+ beings ability to considerably hold more and more light within their dense physical 3D bodies. This accumulation of Christ light is important to the 5D+ being because it is the gateway to the source of pure conscious thought which caused its manifestation. At this point, cosmic awareness begins and the physical being now has access to its life force and can began to project its consciousness to other dimensions.

The ability to project the consciousness of the three- dimensional physical being through the 5D+ consciousness is significant in that a being attains multidimensionality and can traverse through the higher dimensions and create the alignments in synchronicities that will manifest in the physical as emotions, thoughts and actions. For one's multidimensionality work to manifest properly in the desired dimension, space and time must align and synchronize perfectly to set off the sequence of events that begin the cycle of manifestation. The cycle of manifestation is a process whereby, one chooses to either consciously or subconsciously create the reality or realities one desires to experience on their journey of life.

The success of the cycle of manifestation is centered on the ability of the performer to recognize the signs and guides which will direct them towards the emotions that will lead to the thoughts necessary to create further alignments in the external three-dimensional realm. External alignments are achieved when pure intention of the desire affects the thoughts of others whom one will interact with on the 3D physical dimension leading to the manifestation of the intended desire. One can also recruit members of their soul group in the eighth dimension to assist in bringing forth their desires by creating further alignments and synchronicities within their realities that will cross paths with the purpose of the one whose desire brought forth the work for manifestation into the 3D physical reality.

The cycle of manifestation ensues when one reaches a level of consciousness that allows for access to the multidimensional aspect of the being. The multidimensional aspect of the being also known as the soul is a result of the elevation in consciousness of the three-dimensional being to allow for the expansive development of their spatial perception. The expansive development of spatial perception allows for one to increase the perception of space within their environment. As one spatial perception develops, their awareness to self in relation to the physical world becomes distorted or fragmented. Fragmentation occurs to protect the conscious mind from the experience of altering sensitivity to the environment. As one advances through this process, previous memories and emotions are filtered through the developed conscious for reintegration into their prospective places based on increased awareness of self and current understanding of those experiences.

The act of filtering passed memories and feelings is known as passed life regression, a process that involves the retrieval of memories from one's past and clarifying any leftover negative distortions. This filtration process allows one to renew their life force and increase their creative energy. The creative energy that comes from the life force is known as the yin and yang. Yin being the power to do and the yang is being in the space to do. The eleventh dimension is where the yin and yang energy exist, separated by a thin membrane, but always together. Removal of this thin membrane activates the awakening from pure consciousness until its return to source, birthed by the energy exchange between the yin mother and yang father. Yang transduces yin to plant the seed, a zygote is born and can take on any form from spirit to universe.

Above the twelfth dimension is the highest perceptual dimension within the multidimensional space of the manifested being. This dimension is the dimension of pure source that gives birth to pure thought through intent of the Christ or pure creation of light which can also be called the thirteenth dimension allowing for the emanation of source in the twelfth dimension. The source dimension is the pure source of all that is and then some and unconditional love. All that is created is created with these intentions and all that desire to return to source must return to source with these intentions. Ascension and dissension is the traversing through the dimension. Ascension being the rising up from 1 to 12 and dissension the downward movement from 12 to 1.

All emanations of creation start at the source or the void in the twelfth dimension in the conscious of the being from consciousness to formed manifestation, emanations are first released as stellar planetary or universal beings. The emanation cycle continues with formation of consciousness, then projected consciousness, to the soul and spiritual or emotional body followed by the physical body, and finally bodily functions and body make-up. Through careful study of this process, one may be able to recognize the entanglement in how all that manifest in the physical is a consequence of that which was the pure intent of the creator whether consciously or subconsciously at the source.

This notion is what gives rise to my 5D goals theory, this theory affirms that the fifth dimension is the optimal dimension for human evolutionary existence. As beings, holding fifth- dimensional consciousness, we can project our souls into higher or lower levels of consciousness to manifest the things within that realm of existence into the physical 3D realm. One may descend to the lower levels of consciousness to create alignments from that realm such as survival skills to develop coping mechanisms which work to control the emotional body at the neurological level. Also, the lower realms hold the consciousness of bodily functions. One may need to manipulate this realm for healing of the physical body at the cellular level. A third consciousness that exists in the dimensions lower than the third dimension include the subconscious mind. One may seek to reach to manifest conscious thought and may descend to this lower realm to access memories that may be used to manifest thoughts, emotions, and actions in the physical 3D realm.

The dimensions of consciousness that exists above the third dimension are absent of physical manifestation of consciousness. The mental expansion which leads to the increase in spatial perception of one's consciousness, is the pathway for the interactions between the classical worlds with the quantum world. For conceptual purposes, the classical and quantum world can be compared to the micro and macro world, where that the classical world is what we see and know, and quantum is the unseen and rather unknown world. As mental expansion develops within a being, access and awareness to the higher dimensions become more perceptual to the being, as perceptions increase being's power to control these interactions also increase in a mostly linear fashion. Meaning that as time increases, so does space and so does awareness and thus control.

The goal of ascension is to manifest into the third- dimensional consciousness that which is potentiality in the twelfth-dimension consciousness. One who has realized self and is able to manifest into the high consciousness of thought within self has discovered the true power of being, their life force, and their ability to create that which is desired through pure intention. This is the being's divine destiny of all beings to become a powerful creator. Once one realizes their power, they can begin to use their will to resonate on the frequency of the conscious of pure love which always increases the cellular vibration of one towards the Christ or source of pure consciousness. With connection to the source of universal consciousness of the void, one can manipulate the dimensions to create alignments and synchronicities in the three-dimensional reality that assist in accomplishing their realized purpose.

Become A Powerful Creator

CHAPTER ONE
DISCOVERING YOUR PURPOSE

Becoming a powerful creator is life's purpose, but first one must be aware of their power to discover their purpose. Discovery is exposing of something which is concealed due to the lack of one's perception to that which is unknown. Three-dimensional beings lack the power to perceive their purpose and therefore will need to increase their self-awareness since this is a requirement for the development of higher consciousness which will lead to the will to understand and then creates the cellular vibrational frequency required to ascend the being to the higher dimensions connecting with one's soul. The soul is the aspect of the being that will translate one's purpose by way of energetic communications which will be perceived as emotions that become thoughts then actions. This series of actions causes the alignments and synchronicities necessary for the purpose to manifest to the being in the third dimensional reality.

A purpose that has manifested into reality must still be interpreted by the being for interpersonal meaning. All experiences, intentional or coincidental, are pieces of information one uses to understand the language of energy the soul uses to communicate one's purpose. One may say what is revealed is the being's purpose to become a creator and to bestow upon oneself the power to become free of any limitations that prevent the progress towards one purpose of becoming a creator. Upon this revelation, the being can discover how their thoughts are their first creations and are thus able to understand the construct of the creation process and their ability and purpose to create.

Creation is simply the process of manifesting into existence that which is not known to the being to exist. Therefore, new feelings, emotions, thoughts actions or other three-dimensional structures are manifestations or creations of the being experiencing them. This is the process of creation that is revealed to the being by the higher-self. The thought itself is a manifestation of potentialities of realized paradigms where now the being perceives each though as significant and determines whether to further materialize the manifestation into a solid, physical compressed state or to leave it in thought form.

Once one decides to materialize that which doesn't already exist through their intentions based on the awareness of self and will to fulfill one's newly discovered purpose, they have become a powerful creator. What is materialized into the three-dimensional reality was once a formless vision or dream, we all have a vision, a dream, an idea or a small voice communicating to us. What is being articulated to the being from the soul intellect to consciousness of the being's mind is an illustration of that which can potentially be materialized through alignments, synchronicities and the use of one's creative forces.

Often, we feel an express desire to share those abstract thoughts with others and words fall short of our ability to express our observations to others. We strive to reconstruct and materialize our visions into some form others can experience like other structures which materialize in the three-dimensional solid physical reality. The form may be two or three-dimensional. An example of a two-dimensional structure would be a drawing of the one's vision while a three-dimensional structure could a model that replicates one's vision and could potentially be functional with moving parts that can do more work and thus create more power. Thus, perpetuating the cycle of power and creation to other energetic life forms.

The reason one creates is the desire to communicate your observations to others and mere verbal explanations fall short at articulating the being's experience of higher consciousness. You have ineffectively pierced the veil, and the only validation is the manifestation of that which was experienced during one's higher state of consciousness. You have time traveled to a parallel existence in the form of an experienced higher consciousness which is also a state of dimensionality still in the incarnated vessel yet travels interdimensionally using the soul body. When the being is in the soul bod, there is an experience of another version of yourself, a parallel version of oneself that correlates the dimension the soul body manifests in. An example of this soul body manifestation comprehensible would be the three-dimensional being manifesting in the corporeal body. The corporeal body is a condensed form of one's soul body in a low, cellular vibrational frequency state. This lowered, cellular vibrational frequency state causes a decrease in cellular velocity and spatial awareness which leads to a contraction of consciousness.

The expansion of consciousness may be considered as a mental phenomenon without ability to manifest the vision experienced by the being. Therefore, one creates to express that which indwells on the inside of that being's consciousness. Without manifestation of the being's conscious experiences into the physical three-dimensional reality, the existence of the phenomenon of the expansion of consciousness would have no source to confer its validity. Another reason beings create is for the service of their purpose. Each creation emanates a creation that is useful to do some form of energetic work on the dimensional level the creation was manifested in. An example of this is the sun. It is an emanation of the cosmos and serves to bestow energy to the planet earth and all its life forms.

All beings possess the ability to create and possess the potential or latent qualities necessary to manifest with proper development. The development required to manifest takes work and time which produces power, an essential component in the process of ascension, an action that occurs because of conscious expansion. The observer becomes a creator when they can produce their observations for others to see. The observer must feel a strong obligation to produce what was observed. Many times, realizing that their vision serves a purpose to humanity, is the need to force one to use their power to create the alignments and synchronicities that would be needed to progress them towards their purpose of becoming a creator of their vision. The creation is manifested when the observer can design and produce into the three-dimensional reality what was observed in conscious thought.

Creation is simply the manifestation of something doesn't exist, which takes conviction in the belief of what one has seen and their ability to align with that vision to begin to live in that vision. The vision is an aspect of the observers' life, a potential that can manifest if the observer uses their power and will. Therefore, the observer has observed an alternate reality of oneself. The observation of oneself in other dimensions is a phenomenon known as piercing the veil. Piercing the veil allows one to tap into the Akashic records and experience alternate realities of oneself where any of which can be manifested. The Akashic record contains each soul's life force imprint of all one's skills, talents, gifts, and personas and, once discovered, the being can choose which self to align with and live as in the three- dimensional physical reality.

After creation, the being can prove the existence of higher consciousness which allowed for the coming forth of their vision to display your creation for others. The ability for others to experience your creation is what makes one's experience of higher consciousness a reality. Once the being's conscious experience becomes a reality, the creation experienced by one being can be reproduced by other beings using the same or a similar manifestation process. The ability for others to experience our higher consciousness establishes the necessity for all beings to understand and discover the ability to become a powerful creator. This is the reason that we create for the advancement of humanity towards its ultimate purpose of becoming a five-dimensional plus being. A five- dimensional plus being holds the consciousness of the soul in the material world in a state of constant meditation with continuous flow of information and interpretation from source to being. The source being the void of the twelfth dimension, the Christ, or light energy of the life force that produces inception of thought.

Today we can see many examples of creation in the world. Some examples of creation we may not realize came from higher conscious thought to manifest in the physical three-dimensional reality includes songs, videos, poems, books, buildings or structures, vehicles, babies, lifestyles, brands, themes, games or dishes. Each of the examples represent a different area of creation for the mind to conceive for understanding the concept of being a creator and therefore creating simply from by using the power of conscious thought. Creation is power, and beings exist to create with the use of that power which is the quotient of work over time. A being who discovers their wheel and power to create can achieve anything they can conceive. You could be the one to create the paraphernalia of the future.

The devices believed to be mechanically, structurally or functionally impossible, such as a flying vehicle, absolute sustainable energy, vital communication devices, the next app, the next diet that prolongs life and cures disease, the next shoe that we will never wear, the next genre of music, only the observer knows what was observed and what one will have the will to manifest. Humanity needs, all beings to discover their ability to become a powerful creator to bring forth an economy of unity. Unity helps to foster more creation and each creation and creator do more work over time and produce more power.

CHAPTER TWO
ALIGN WITH YOUR PURPOSE

Manifestation altogether concerns alignments and synchronicities. The alignments first need to develop a being's awareness for a conscious expansion to become multidimensional. The distinctive alignments required to produce synchronicities in the physical, with people, places, and things will supply one with the means of accomplishing their purpose without the limitations of the physical world. The alignment is frequency, space, time consciousness, and will. These aspects of alignment increase awareness of the soul, which is the multidimensional aspect of one's self. Together with the synchronicities one can align with their purpose.

One's purpose is the reason it exists. It's a job one must do. The visions are communicated from the higher consciousness as dreams with the potential to be manifested as a big idea, which becomes the vision of the powerful creator. One's purpose will be truly desired by the heart. When a being experiences increased spatial awareness, it is a state of meditation which sanctions the occurrence of vivid dreams that will be experienced by the smart body. The smart body is the mechanism by which sensory of thought is communicated to the three- dimensional physical being. This communication is a sixth sense and allows the physical body to use its five physical senses to perceive their observations and use those sensory communications as force to will in the vision with the creative power. Together the aligning of this force, will, and power, one begins to develop a potential gift and uses that gift to manifest into existence their dreams, vision and purpose.

The being's ability to align with the synchronicities that abounds access to the source through a multidimensional experience disconnects one from the ego. The ego is an aspect of the being that disconnects one from the universal consciousness. The ego wants to have personal experience and needs these experiences to interpret the world. Awareness to the world is based on experiences, thoughts, feelings and faculty of consciousness. The three- dimensional physical body – eyes, ears, nose, mouth, head, chest, arms, and legs or corporeal body - is what the ego uses for this experience. Since the ego lives one life time after death, the memories of that entity cease to exist except as an imprint on the universal consciousness of the soul. This is the aspect of the being that is mourned in death since the soul aspect of the being continues forward in the Akash. The reason one may seem impatient in life, tirelessly needing to do things quickly and figure it out in one lifetime, because there is no coming back for the ego.

Once the being disconnects from the ego and experiences conscious expansion, one is then able to connect to the universal consciousness of oneness. The universal consciousness is the Akashic record the being used to receive thought through the soul aspect of the being. This communication utilizing the smart body can create multidimensional experiences with potential paradigms not known by the three-dimensional world. It no longer needs the ego aspect of the being to create three- dimensional physical experiences. The soul aspect of the being contrary to the ego creates experiences using wisdom and does not live in the creation of the experience but lives in the experience of the creation.

One's soul is a spiritual body of the resurrected

body, a celestial body fitted for the wants of the spirit, conformed to a spiritual life at resurrection or rebirth of consciousness. The rebirth of consciousness allows the spiritual body to access higher conscious thoughts and feel increased awareness based on wisdom, rather than empirical knowledge, collectivist thought, moral thought, high quality of awareness and understanding. One's spirit is patient, understands that what is focused on will be manifested when the power is sufficient for that frequency and vibration. Fortunately, the spirit has lived multiple lifetimes with its Akashic information that is passed down from generation to generation from the beginning of creation.

Soul and ego are contrasting aspects of one's self where the soul lives to become a powerful creator and the ego exists to live in the experience of creation. Because the soul has access to the Akashic records, one who is connected to their soul has awakened to the realization that the being still has unfinished business unlike the ego subsists on wasting and having an enjoyable time. Conceptual communication through the smart body to be perceived by the heart is how the soul assists one in realizing their purpose. The ego starves the being into survival mode in an unconscious state of adaptation to the external environment. The egos influence over the being and disconnects one from the source and into an unconscious primal state or beast mode. On the other hand, the soul operates on innate intelligence which is the connection to the universal consciousness that stores the blueprint for each being's purpose.

Soul is the aspect of self that unites being and purpose. For one to have access to the soul aspect of self, one must first be reborn. The rebirth is of the spirit or conscious into an increased expansive state of awareness. After rebirth, the spirit and the being are one and manifest as the soul aspect of one's self. The soul then becomes the being's guide through life. Due to limitations of the physical three- dimensional reality, total integration occurs over time at different rates for different beings. Lag in integration creates the necessity for the being to accept the soul aspect of self as one's guide because the being will still experience fragmented ego aspects of self which may cause the being to lose touch with their power to become a creator.

The relationship between the being and the soul aspect of self requires an enormous amount of trust. The being will need to learn to trust the communications received through the smart body and the higher consciousness and its ability to interpret and download that information to one's physical mind. The download's that are received come through a conscious, meditative state and present as dreams or visions to the being. The meditative state activates one's innate deoxyribonucleic acid system and causes the smart body to communicate with means of enhancing integration to the being such as change in taste to more energetic foods. Also, the need for increased amounts of rest is required to maintain one's energy levels as well for parallel travel and for further higher conscious downloads in order to maintain vibration on the frequency of unconditional love.

Full integration of the soul and transformation into spirit yields a fifth dimension plus beings. Becoming 5D+ being is one's goal and the meditative states that one experiences are designed to contribute to the success of the process. Therefore, the more one connects to soul, the more one connects to the source, their purpose, their power, the universal conscious and the Akashic record. The integration progress is necessary to protect the data being downloaded to the soul from reaching the ego. The ego cannot be trusted with such wisdoms as the soul because the ego is selfish and will only use the ego to further enhance the experiences the ego has within. In contrast, the soul understands that its purpose is to become a powerful creator.

For one to experience their purpose, one must first be aligned with destiny. Alignment allows for synchronizations of events which allow for the manifestation you were born to create to uplift humanity. Your destiny is not a location, but an action that happens to the fifth dimension plus being expressed as a thought that exist in paradigms with multiple potentials which can be manifested at the will. All things work together for those who believe and all events that one experiences are alignments with a purpose to synchronize one with phases in the process of working to manifest a vision and all these events have significance, the good and the ugly. For a being to align with purpose, one must constantly stay focused on that which one desires to create or their purpose.

The secret to becoming a powerful creator is for one to allow one's heart to be the guide to initiating your synchrony destinies. Synchrony Destinies are synchronizations of places and time which lead one towards one's destiny of being a powerful creator. It is about living in purpose. Creators create and what one creates will serve the world. Each one must ask of one's self what creation does their creative spirit align with. What one chooses to align their creative spirit towards is what will manifest. One must not limit one's purpose because of glamour, fame, riches, or support. A real purpose will be received by the world in its time and place and the job of the creator is simply to create.

CHAPTER THREE
CONFIRM YOUR PURPOSE

Once one aligns with purpose, the process of confirming one's purpose ensues. The process of confirming one's purpose includes many checks and balances that are used to validate one's experiences as the process of creation evolves until manifestation of that which was observed while the being was in a state of higher conscious thought. One who is genuinely working to make headway in manifesting what they are destined to create will be aware of alignments as they occur, and beings are thus able to synchronize these alignments to their destiny to become a powerful creator. Synchronizations of these alignments requires strict accuracy. The accuracy is corroborated in the three- dimensional physical reality verified through conceptual communication that supports the being confirming the truthfulness of one's purpose.

Validation of purpose can be confirmed through feelings or thoughts communicated to the smart body with multiple potential for manifestation into the three-dimensional physical reality. For a being to learn the language the smart body communicates in, the being goes through a process of substantiating the communication by checking the accuracy of previous alignments to one's purpose. During this process, one must determine worthiness of purpose and if one can match one's identity to the identity of the self that will fulfill the purpose. Once a being begins to self-identify with one's purpose, one must verify the ability to accomplish the purpose by using the power one is equipped especially for the manifestation of the being's purpose. One who is connected to the soul learns to trust the power one has to become a powerful creator and thus that force to manifest one's vision.

Synchronicities exist to guide one towards their purpose, synchronicities are events that occur at the same time, yet seem disconnected. Alignments are encountered through these synchronicities. One who can accurately cohobate the events that are occurring simultaneously through alignments in the three-dimensional physical world. A being with purpose experiences peace which allows the soul to use various methods to download the purpose of the being into the three-dimensional conscious.

49

Often the downloads one received are corroborated by another physical being as part of the collective conscious which allows others to see into their vision because the other being is either directly or indirectly related to the purpose to be manifested.

Many alignments are necessary and must occur to cause a place and time to convene in the physical, a graceful being is given protection by the spirit world as one works to accomplish the soul's purpose. The assistance from the spirit world comes from one's soul mates, from their soul group which was manifested in the eighth dimension of the being's existence. Through pure intention only is the soul's purpose fulfilled. Nothing can stop the fulfillment of that purpose because all things will work together for those who believe in the power to create.

Once a being's purpose has been confirmed, the work necessary to manifest takes precedence over all other activities the being either enjoys or is obligated to in life. Great attention is given to the details of the process of manifesting one's purpose and a plan to make sure the process is successfully developed. As the being begins to work through the process of manifestation, alignments and synchronicities in the physical begin to occur to move one along in the process of manifestation. Alignments are caused by the being following the higher conscious soul guide or intuition to meet up with places, people, or things which will be synchronized to create a parallel of events in the seen and unseen worlds. The synchronizing of these parallel events will assist the being in manifesting one's purpose into physical, experiential existence and it is very important in manifestation because it is the bringing together or aligning of these energies in various combinations that yield one's desires to be manifested from higher conscious thought into the physical three-dimensional realm. Therefore, one who has confirmed the purpose of life will always seem to be at the right place and at the right time. Nothing is a coincidence in this being's cycle of existence. A purposeful being will always have what is needed to accomplish tasks that assist in the fulfillment of that purpose and through the laws of attraction will feel drawn to those triggers of manifestation. That is how a being acquires the physical material possessions necessary to accomplish one's purpose.

All beings have a unique purpose to fulfill in life. Many people may have similar purposes with varying, subtle differences depending on the fulfillment of that purpose. Many times, what is manifested for some doesn't serve others and therefore variability in manifestations comes from each being's individual, distinct experience with the physical three-dimensional world. That variation of experience in a similar event leads to variation in the manifestations which will fulfill the same purpose or achieve the same paradigm from a different potentiality. No one's purpose is insignificant and all are used for the progression of the human species towards attaining 5D+ consciousness.

As beings with 5D+ consciousness, all beings will be in a constant state of construction and destruction due to instant manifestations through thoughts. These beings will be fully aware of what each manifestation represents in the process of the evolution of manifestation and use the energy from all potential manifestation to create one's purpose rather than wasting energy to determine whether the manifestation was significant or not. One must remain focused on the purpose one wishes to fulfill when creating because the energy is consumed to align every detail needed to manifest one's purpose and if the energies are not properly aligned the frequency for manifestation of a particular creation will not occur and one must start over with the process of fulfilling that purpose paying close attention to the details which will be required to accomplish the goal needed to progress one in the process of creation and manifestation of one's purpose.

The vision of purpose is designed to be fulfilled and getting there is determined by how accurately you align to the synchronicities that guide you to your purpose. While progressing through the process of manifestation, one must ask if this process of accomplishing the purpose will be confirmed in the interactions of the alignments in a flowing manner, the path of least resistance, or the resistance causing the synchronicities not to occur and prevents the physical manifestation of one's purpose. Something small could be slightly off and the being may need to meditate constantly to realign and reconfirm directions for synchronicities as one work towards the fulfillment of one's purpose.

Verification of one's purpose is evidenced by the accuracy of purpose that presents itself as proof through manifestation from higher dimensional thought to lower three-dimensional physical reality. Some beings experience visual verification as the launching of manifestation of one's purpose and the accuracy of the visions presented to the being are confirmed by their effectiveness in serving humanity. Other beings may have communication of purpose through inspired thought such as seeing a color or awkward movement. One's environment stands as the evidence which will verify the validity of the manifestation of one's purpose. That was a manifested form of communication from the higher conscious thought dimensions by its ability to affect what initially inspired the being to create what one was originally moved to form into the three-dimensional physical reality.

Dreams are one of the most familiar forms of communication used by the higher conscious thought dimensions to convey one's purpose for manifestation into the three-dimensional physical reality. Dreams occur as one enters an altered state of consciousness brought on by physiological substances such as melatonin which cause one to fall into a subconscious or sleep state. In this state, there is a disconnection from the corporeal, physical body and the being travels by way of the astral body. The astral body is a subtle body that has form yet no physical three- dimensional structure. In this state, the being can experience parallel paradigms in which one experiences themselves living in one's purpose. Through this experience, the being may materialize into reality with proper alignment and synchronize the events that occurred during the being's dream state.

Another form of verification which confirms one's purpose is the amount of reprieve one receives to assist with the fulfillment and manifestation of that being's purpose. This means that one working to fulfill and manifest their purpose will be honored in function by always acquiring what is needed, where it's needed, and from whom it's needed, when it's needed. And these needs are fulfilled regardless of limitations that may exist in the physical three-dimensional world such as time, finances, and other resources necessary for the actualization of one's purpose.

Some may have the validity of the purpose one is to manifest communicated by having inadvertent alignments and synchronicities that allow a self-actualized being to materialize one's purpose purely through intention. Things just seem to happen for one on this path of creation because of the ability to discern confirmations from other beings, time, places and signs along the journey of actualization of one's purpose. These confirmations alone supply the being with the proper amount of captivation to be motivated intrinsically and not require outside help or encouragement to become a powerful creator.

According to the twelfth-dimensional model, the twelfth dimension is where the creative conscious dwells and is manifested as conceptual thought in the ninth dimension down to actualized thought in the fifth dimension. From actualized thoughts, the being can then conceptually view the thought in the fourth dimension and further physically reproduce that thought in the third dimension with the necessary alignments and synchronicities that will bring about the manifestation of one's creative conscious which serves to validate the process of creation as given by the creator. Confirmation of purpose is difficult for the conscious in the physical form and the being must project their astral, ethereal soul body into the higher dimensions placing the physical body in an unconscious state. The sleep state of the physical being is necessary for the transfer of consciousness from a physical form into the form required to enter the higher dimensions thus leaving the physical body insensible, in a sleep or unconscious condition.

The fifth dimension is where the actualized thoughts, or self of the being is located, that is why becoming a 5D+ being is important for one who is to become a powerful creator. The 5D+ being is an individual with a physical body that can project into the fifth dimension of reality while in an alert state. This may also be a form of meditation which is the expression of high conscious thoughts which may be achieved by a highly disciplined individual. The discipline of this being bestows upon them ascending mastery into integration of the soul, the spirit, or the will and the self.

The soul self is the physical self in fifth-dimensional consciousness. Integration with the physical results in a 5D+ being able to see works and righteousness which brings forth the will to access creative conscious to instantly manifest into actualized thought. The 5D+ being can then physically manifest that thought directly into a three-dimensional reality for others to experience and verify the creation. And the creation that exist is that which was brought forth by the creator was achieved through meditation. Becoming a 5D+ being is a crucial step to becoming a powerful creator. Through mediation, the being can project the soul aspect of self into the higher dimension where alignments and synchronicities necessary in the three-dimensional world can be established while still in a conscious state. This enhancement to the three- dimensional being as evidenced above allows for the being to experience actualized thought or dreams while in a conscious state and confirm one's creative power.

Once the being confirms the creative power that can be attained as a 5D+ being, the true self is realized, the conscious and subconscious mind have begun to partner up to put the being on track to become a powerful creator. Due to the integration of the conscious and subconscious mind, the being can begin to experience peace and harmony. They will start to understand the knowledge and power possessed through one's DNA is activated through accessing of the collective consciousness and the experience of oneness that comes to the 5D+ being. The plus in the 5D+ being stands for the multidimensionality that one possesses which will allows for the being to be in control of one's own destiny.

The realization of self leads to drastic life changes for the now 5D+ being. Recognizable changes in attitude, health, perception, perspective, knowledge, spirituality, moral, mood, demeanor, grace and anything that edifies you towards a more positive direction thus clearing the junk that inhibited the increase in your cellular vibrational frequency required to access the higher conscious mind. These changes lead to the development of will and ultimately allowed the being to become a powerful creator.

CHAPTER FOUR

AFFIRM YOUR PURPOSE

The being that has yielded to their authenticity, genuineness and inspiration of purpose affirms the validity of their purpose during the multidimensional integration process. During the multidimensional integration process, the realization of self occurs, and the being begins to act in a way that expresses and affirms the being's knowledge of one's true self. As the physical being integrates with the soul self to become the 5D+ being, communication with the higher self allows for action of works and the affirmation of one's power to create evidenced by the being's manifestations into the three-dimensional reality.

The 5D+ being further affirms one is on track with the purpose for one's life. The reason is because the being is in a state of self-awareness. They are conscious of the experiences the soul journey to retrieve and the thoughts that will be manifested into the physical reality, either abstractly or concretely. The awareness of the presence of the soul guides higher conscious thoughts, allows the being to experience the creation process, and the power one possesses to create from the void to conceptual then actualized thoughts and three-dimensional manifestations.

Once the being is in a state of constant awareness of the self and the soul guide, the declaration can be expressed by the beings' realization of the true self and understanding that one is what one chooses to be by declaring "I am" whatever the being has declared to be. The being declares through affirmation of physical manifestation that the being is a powerful creator. A covenant is framed between the physical self and the soul self that accesses the higher consciousness and requires that the physical self-utilize this awareness only in the pursuit of purpose to prevent the malevolent use of these forcible creative powers.

Undertaking this new oath, the being understands that the power to create has been bestowed upon the being for the objective of fulfilling one's purpose. A purpose which once fully manifested stands to serve to be beneficial to humanity. A being that has affirmed the purpose for one's life establishes a bond with the universe to work in synchronicity to bring about that which one was destined to discover, the power to create. This bond is evidenced by the being's ability to overcome difficult circumstances and navigate through their journey with an elevated level of problem solving skills. Because of the ability one has to travel to higher dimensions to create the necessary alignments and synchronicities this will lead one to triumph in the three-dimensional reality when faced with obstacles that stand to prevent one from the progression of one's purpose.

Affirming one's purpose is a process determined by circumstances and life situations if progressing on the right life path. A path that will lead to the fulfillment of one's purpose. Affairs that occurs in life are of no coincidence, but are lessons meant to bring the being into the realization, actualization, and state of constant self- awareness. This includes awareness of feelings that are transmitted through the gut. Discernment of emotions travel through the heart and understanding of thought that is transmitted through the brain. The being's sensitivity to judging these actions allows the being to interpret the information which is being downloaded from the conceptual consciousness through the smart body to be actualized in the physical as an abstract message.

The one receiving the abstract message uses intuition or instincts to decipher the message so that it may be explained orally, written down, or expressed in another artistic or creative method to be perceived in the three-dimensional physical reality. Once the being can effectively communicate with the smart body, everything begins to come together in a sensible manner that functions to allow the being to see that one thing did or did not happen so that another thing could or could not happen. This is the beginning of the being's constant state of self-awareness as well as alignments and synchronicities manifesting in the physical reality which were orchestrated on the higher dimensions for the fulfillment of one's purpose.

The fulfillment of one's purpose will require one to declare without doubt that the wisdom being received is authentic. This authentication is accomplished by the establishment of trust between the being and the source of wisdom. The beings start to act on the messages to the extent that what was expected to occur due to the information received in the message is the actual event that occurred based on the information received in the message with acceptable variations that don't change the ultimate expected outcome of events or occurrences.

After one has affirmed the purpose communicated to the being to be fulfilled, the purpose and the identity of that purpose, in fact, belongs to that being. For example, a being that affirms their ability to heal by healing, can in fact, identify as a healer. Once the identity of the being is affirmed, one must begin to live in a constant state of awareness of that purpose and identify as oneself as the operative for that purpose. This allows the being to develop the expected persona in the future upon full maturation of the higher self within the being. Commitment to the fulfillment of one's purpose is demonstrated by the consistent undertaking of the task necessary to manifest one's purpose into physical reality. Doing this allows one to affirm their purpose by experiences, day dreams, visions, fantasies, and conceptual communications that lead to the expected and intended manifestations in the three-dimensional reality.

Once the being affirms their identity as a 5D+ being, manifestation occurs as mentioned earlier in this chapter. The being understands the agreement that has been established between the lower and higher selves and pledges to trust the higher self as the guide for one's life journey. The being immediately establishes the purpose to be fulfilled, then a system of rules is organized that the being will strictly adhere to including habits of meditation, discernment, diet, morals, or what is right in one's heart, patience, and other practices the soul deems necessary for that being.

For the being to determine what practices the soul deems necessary, the being will need to establish a truthfulness of purpose. The establishment of truthfulness of purpose requires one to be honest with oneself about one's feelings, thoughts, and emotions that are to be experienced from a diverse source of stimuli. Those thoughts, feelings, and emotions are to be processed in a way that creates insight into the being's true self. The more knowledge of true self, the more discovery of moral understanding by what is experienced in the physical as an abstract message communicated to the being for that being to understand.

The being is being guided to learn how to always be true to one's self. It is this guide of truthfulness that will allow the being to make the right choices under any circumstances following the directions and messages of their guides. Once the being begins to recognize the purpose that is to be fulfilled, it can be of surprise to the being. The being has affirmed through alignments and synchronicities that the journey one has followed has been one on the journey towards fulfillment of that purpose. The being trusts that to continue of the path of the guide is right without regard to if that being's purpose will bring about riches, fame, or any other worldly glories. The being must also trust the journey that seems bigger than what the being has the capacity to manifest.

At this point, one begins to realize that the fulfillment of purpose is a lifetime journey in which one is continually progressing on as one takes actions towards manifesting that purpose. The right actions are interpreted by the being from the source and lead to alignments and synchronicities that moves one forward. If the being is unable to take the right action, for whatever reason, the being receives a set of alignments and synchronicities that sends the being through to repeat the lesson until the right choice is made. The goal is that eventually the being will understand that building the truthfulness of purpose is an important part of the process on the road to the fulfillment of that purpose. The right choice becomes like a sign that the being learns to pay attention to as one's moral sensitivity increases. It is moral sensitivity that allows one to be more in sync with one's internal time and allows for alignments and synchronicities to occur on the timeline in which they are appointed to manifest.

Most of a being's lifetime is plagued with thoughts and desires of doing something great or something special and that is because it is the soul's desire to manifest one's purpose by becoming a powerful creator. Learning that the ability to manifest one's purpose births knowledge of self. Knowledge of self allows the being to understand the means to produce the purpose that is to be fulfilled. This is done with personality, charisma, moral, intellect and many external and internal agents that with the use of mental or emotional authority bend to the users will. For the being to get the desired results of the expected manifestations that will be brought into the three-dimensional reality, there needs to be a significant investment in the amount of time spent on practicing with the abilities one possesses to manifest ideas into the three-dimensional reality.

Beings should begin to perfect their creative powers and understand how to use the means in which they possess for bringing forth their manifestation into the physical reality. The being is responsible for continuing to live a disciplined, benevolent life, making decisions based on the rightness of the response to be fulfilled rather what one wants to do without regard to one's feelings about that which is being done. These are the aspects of the being that allows for deciding the right response. What gives the being the ability to choose the right response are virtues, they are generally held by beings with high moral standing and that can be entrusted with such knowledge as to not to use its power to destroy.

Beings with the power to create may use a creation process that helps bring forth expected manifestations. One of the steps of the creation process is awareness. One must be aware that every thought and action dictates whether the being is able to manifest the expected creation based on the being's ability to constantly live in every moment and to constantly be cognizant of the work that is being done to be directed by the higher conscious. Because beings are developing spiritual aptitude always, there may be moments where the connection to the source is broken and the being subconsciously begins to act in one's own will until an event occurs that reconnects the being to source. The disconnection between the being and source, for whatever amount of time, causes missed alignments and synchronicities in the physical reality and set the being backwards on the fulfillment of purpose.

A being that is set back on the fulfillment of purpose can suffer severe detriment to the continued progression towards one purpose for that lifetime. That is why it is imperative for beings to constantly track the progress one is making towards fulfillment of purpose. The being must self-check and self-correct constantly by creating an internal feedback loop. The internal feedback loop would possibly consist of a stimuli and response design. The stimuli and response design could consist of a question that would stimulate the being to respond with an answer. For example, a healer could track whether the work being done is healing and the same for an engineer and so on.

One must be extremely focused on the fulfillment of purpose even with the distractions of life on the physical three-dimensional reality. There must be a constant self- reminder that the being was created to manifest the being's purpose. This causes the being to remember that there is a cycle that is taking place that maintains order and the continuance of life in the physical reality. Every creation must continue the cycle of creation. In this aspect, the being is almost machine-like, always and constantly collecting, processing and analyzing data.

The good thing about machines is the reliability of duplication of desired results, so, if one is to use the same system for every step towards the progression of the fulfillment of purpose, the being will always be in alignment for obtaining the desired or expected result to occur or manifest. The process of a being's machine may work as follows: The first step in the process after the being is a powerful creator and the architect of the purpose that is to be fulfilled may be drafting. Once the purpose is drafted, one can begin to collect the necessary resources to bring forth what is to be manifested. After the being has identified what is necessary to manifest the purpose to be fulfilled, the being can begin the design, taking into account how the creation will positively affect humanity and how it will be perceived or experienced by the world. There are many formats for presenting physical manifestations including oral, written abstract art, music, performance or an object. The desired type of manifestation will depend on how the being chooses to express the creation in the physical reality.

The design of the purpose assists the being in the next step which is the shaping of purpose and that includes experimenting with methods of delivering the desired manifestation to humanity with the intended effect. Intention is a very crucial key in the process of manifestation. For it is intention that allows the being to bend the universe to the will of the being's desire to allow one's creations to manifest. Finally, once intention is initiated, the construction of purpose can begin. This is one of the most important parts of the manifestation process. The construction portion of the manifestation process is where the being begins to do work in the physical to encounter the alignments that will lead to the synchronicities necessary for the being to physically present the manifestation to the world. And the manifestation is then to be used in the world to be experienced by humanity.

The state of constant awareness and living in the moment as it relates to the being's purpose requires persistent following of effort necessary for the advancement of the unique character one is destined to grow into to. Also, extreme focus on these activities gives rise to the cycle's perpetual prompting of this internal feedback loop. The internal feedback loop transfigures the system that gives rise to the machine-like repetitions of continuous data processing and analyzing of external and internal stimuli both physical and instinctual. It is at this point that the being is ready to begin to live in the purpose that is destined to be fulfilled and become a powerful creator.

CHAPTER FIVE

LIVE IN YOUR PURPOSE

The process of becoming a powerful creator can successfully accomplished by anyone who chooses to do the required work necessary to possess such power. For one to command such power one must first be able to command one's self. Self is the external and internal environment in which awareness of self opens the gateway to the journey of becoming a powerful creator. The journey of becoming a powerful creator begins with the alignments that lead to the discovery of purpose. Realizing one's purpose requires an introspective process of self-reflection, self-realization, self-awareness and your state of being. This is the alignment with consciousness to time and space all of which exist in the physical and unseen force. Your state of being is recognized as an unseen place connecting to a physical time and space with awareness being your ability to perceive this location minus its third-dimensional physical representation.

Once the being begins the process of realizing the purpose that is to be fulfilled, the beings will drive the onset of the crucial actions that will bring about the discovery of purpose that will lead to the alignment of purpose, which initiates the confirmation of purpose that kicks off the affirmation of purpose and commences when the being is living in the purpose that was destined to be fulfilled and has become a powerful creator.

At the point when the being is living in depth of purpose, the being realizes that the process of becoming a powerful creator is not a random one, but fate. The birthright of the individual that experiences its conceptualization, which is manifested as actualized thought, can be interpreted by the being. The interpretation by the being will depend on convictions specific to that individual and understanding comes from victories one achieves on the journey of life. With intellectual comprehension, understanding becomes knowledge that when applied becomes wisdom. Wisdom is timeless information that allows one in a state of high awareness to realize it is the individual's destiny to fulfill one's purpose.

Many beings fail to manifest the purpose to be fulfilled in that individual's lifetime because of uncleared, karmic debt. Often times, beings desire to create a new reality when the reality that is currently being experienced has not yet been reconciled. The current reality consists of the present and past tense selves the soul has experienced. This unreconciled reality causes karmic debt in the being's life. When a being is indebted to the karmic cycle, the conceptualized thoughts will be experienced by the being with the lack of understanding to form knowledge. An acquired knowledge which can then be applied as the wisdom needed to create the alignments and synchronicities that would progress one towards the fulfillment of that individual's purpose. In principle, this leads one to experience an elusive sense of purpose that can leave one filling empty and gloomy, living in an obscure existence.

Individuals that have worked to reconcile their past by method of passed life regression or some similar process can begin to wholly connect to the higher self that bestows one with the ability to become a powerful creator. These individuals have cleared their karmic debt by facing the obstacles of the lower self which attaches to the ego and causes the detachment from the soul as the being builds a fiercer connection to ego. This is the cause for the elusiveness in those with uncleared, karmic debt. The disconnection that is felt by the being to higher conscious is due to the relationship between the being and the ego as opposed to the spirit. The ego and spirit resist or repel one another and as a result whichever mind the being resolves to will dictate the reality that the being can understand or perceive due to the limited construct of paradigms that exist in the dimensions below the fourth and fifth dimensions and to a small degree, the third dimension, but none lower.

Balance is the ultimate goal for the integration process of the spirit and the three-dimensional human being and that balance is what the 5D+ being embodies. A 5D+ being is one who has realized that there is a purpose to life and begins to do the work to reconcile the individual's past so that one can be allowed to progress towards the fulfilment of one's purpose. In the environment of integration, the being is faking the life of the new being while making the life of the new being by doing the work until the work reaches the realization and actualization occurs. At this point, the being can exist in the physical with ego under submission of the intense connection of the being to the soul. Now, the being has begun to achieve the level of consciousness necessary for the integration process to take place.

A successful integration pathway is the being's destiny or birthright. Every being has a purpose for existing and expresses this uniqueness as a talent of creation. The being creates conceptually, through actualized ideas that become plans that if followed will manifest specific desires. The manifestation of these desires is the actualization of the being's ability to create and when this capability is observed by others, there is a spark of inspiration to discover the individual's' potential of becoming a powerful creator. The most attractive aspect observed by others living in the fulfillment of one's purpose is the joy, contentment and aura of peace among many other positive aspects of the self that the being projects out to the universe. This projection is received by other beings and entities that resonate on the frequency of the power that was put forth.

One living a life of purpose will experience moments of bliss due to the harmony between the universe and the being through higher consciousness. This harmony is owed to the alignments one needs of self to bring forth the higher consciousness that serves as a constant connection between the source of higher consciousness and the being. Being perpetually connected to the source allows one to access energy that allows one to create the synchronicities and alignments created by the being's power. Power is the wavelength over the frequency times Planck's constant.

Therefore, to change the energy of a thing, one must vary the wavelength and frequency of their consciousness to match the frequency of that which is to be manifested. This concept of frequency matching can be likened to tuning the station on the radio. Suppose you want to play a station at 106.1 hertz, the unit of frequency and you want to tune into is playing on a station with a frequency of 102.9 hertz. To tune into to the new station, one would have to turn the dial on the radio until it matches the frequency of the station the being is wanting to tune into. Once the dial and the stations are aligned on the radio, the broadcast can be tuned into and that broadcast is the manifestation of matching those frequencies.

Varying the wavelength is a more difficult concept to actualize into words, like frequency, it is also invisible, and most beings aren't aware of how wavelength affects their environment. But one example that can possibly articulate this complex concept is color. Most beings perceive a certain color at a specific angle of refraction of the eye. For instance, blue is at one spot on the spectrum of the wavelength with a longer wave form, which is the length of the wave that is formed from the energy emitted that caused the perception of the presence of color in the environment to occur. One way to use your power is to use color. Color can change the wavelength and, therefore, the power to create or manifest what was desired.

Becoming a powerful creator is every being's destiny and will occur in one lifetime or another, the choice of which lifetime is up to the being. Ultimately, the power will be ascertained at some point on the being's journey and the conceptual thoughts of one's purpose can be actualized, one thought and one action at a time. Some beings may take longer to come to the actualization of the purpose that is to be fulfilled because of unresolved, karmic debt. It is nearly impossible to begin a new life without first reconciling the fallacies of the previous life. This idea can be conveyed in one lifetime by one choosing to start a new life path within the same lifetime. Issues arise when those matters from the previous life path resurface and unsettle and destroy the foundation of your new life path.

A being with unresolved, karmic debt or unreconciled pasts will experience a sense of detachment from the spiritual aspect of self from birth. This being will need to develop self-awareness through life experiences that will work to begin to align one with the higher consciousness in each of the individual's lifetimes. Because the being is born detached from the soul or spiritual aspect of self, the individual is unconscious to the true self and thus cannot connect to the higher consciousness needed to experience the power of multidimensionality. Since the detached being is unconscious to the multidimensional nature, every experience is perceived as coincidence rather than series of synchronistic alignments. Without the consciousness of multidimensionality, one is unable to communicate with their soul guide and struggles to realize the purpose for that individuals' life.

Living a life of purpose can be very difficult when one cannot make the necessary connections with the higher conscious thoughts, necessary to manifest conceptualized thoughts into actualized thought. With proper action, one can work to bring about what the creators desires to create. Without the ability to translate conceptualized thought into actualized thought, the being cannot create the necessary alignments and synchronicities to bring about the manifestation of that being's purpose. Yet, even with accumulated, karmic debt the being that desires to live a life of purpose, will begin to have experiences that will guide one towards a life path that will begin to reconcile the past karmic debt of that individual and simultaneously allow connections to the higher consciousness.

If the being remains in a state of being that allows for connection to the higher consciousness, the being can begin to work towards the alignments that will resolve karmic debt and usually this allowance is benevolence.

Living a benevolent life is the being's choice and that is a choice to do good above all. Many times, this state of being comes secondary to some traumatic life experience or event that lead the being into a state of reflection and redirection that would bring about a new, more desirable beginning to that being's life. With trial and error, the being can use any acquired knowledge and evidence from life experiences to decide that a benevolent life path is one that will lead the being to the life which is desired.

In some cases, a being is reborn after a lifetime of clearing karmic debt and will come into existence with a sense of self and an early onset of self-awareness. This individual being born relatively clear of karmic debt, is a conscious being with an early onset of vague awareness of multidimensionality. Because of this subtle awareness of multidimensionality, the being can connect with the soul aspect of the self and communicate with the higher consciousness early on in life. Being able to communicate with the soul is a vital aspect in an individual being able to manifest the purpose one is to fulfil. While others may struggle to reach a harmonious relationship with the soul aspect of the self, those beings with cleared, karmic debt are able to communicate with the soul aspect of a being's life early on and begin creating the alignments and synchronicities that will bring about the fulfillment of one's purpose to become a powerful creator.

There are four central, differentiating purposed philosophies between clear versus elusive, karmic debt. One of those differentiating philosophies is purpose. Those born with cleared, karmic debt have a keen sense of purpose as opposed to those born with unresolved, karmic debt. Being's born with unresolved, karmic debt have a weakened sense of purpose and may have so little sense of self that it limits the individual's ability to self-identify. The ability to self-identify is a process that leads to self- awareness, a necessary evolution of the human being to connect to the high consciousness of self.

Another differentiating philosophy concerning clear and unresolved, karmic debt is one's life path. Individuals born with clear, karmic debt are set out on an obvious path in life. For example, one that is born with the ability to play the piano will be a musician or the one that has a keen sense of building things becomes an engineer. As opposed to being born with unresolved, karmic debt that results in blockages that prevent the individual from realizing the path that would allow for the fulfillment of one's purpose, leading to the next differentiating philosophy. That differentiating philosophy is alignment to purpose. Individuals born with cleared, karmic debt will have the ability to create the necessary alignments and synchronicities that would align one with the path that would lead to the fulfillment of that being's purpose. As opposed to individuals with unresolved, karmic debt that are unable to create the necessary alignments and synchronicities that would lead one to the fulfillment of purpose. This causes that being to fruitlessly wonder about the meaning of life.

The final differentiating philosophy is the ability to directly interpret conceptual thought into actualized thought. Being born with cleared, karmic debt allows one immediate access to the higher conscious of the self which uses information from past experiences to interpret the thought. Individuals with unresolved, karmic debt lack the ability to clearly connect to the higher conscious and thus cannot perceive the conceptual thoughts as needing to be interpreted and pass them off as mere, lucid dreams. This inability to interpret conceptualized thought is the most important, potentially-limiting factors in one's ability to become a powerful creator.

Becoming a powerful creator requires recognizing the ability one holds to fulfill the ordained purpose for that being's life. Fulfillment of purpose comes through realization of the self amid actualized thoughts interpreted from conceptual thoughts of the higher-conscious self. The realization of the purpose that one is to fulfill in one lifetime or another is a potential of many the being may choose to manifest. The individual continuously receives conceptual thoughts from the higher consciousness of the self to be actualized with the proper actions. This step brings about the necessary alignments and synchronicities so that any of the conceptualized thoughts can be actualized by the being for realization. The being exercises free will in choosing which conceptual thoughts to actualize and many times this choice may be limited by life experience. Therefore, they may not be able to bring about a desired potential because of many limiting factors in the being's physical reality.

The potential for a being to realize the purpose that is to be fulfilled during one's lifetime or another is loosely constructed on the supposition that the individual knows what purpose is. Once the being becomes aware of oneself, even if only faintly, connection to the higher self is initiated and the individual begins to feel obligated to a vague desire of the heart. At this point, the being has discovered there is a purpose for all of life, even though the being may not be aware of the specific purpose that individual exist to fulfill. Although, the being is aware and motivated by this desire of the heart to find and fulfill that purpose. So, essentially the individual realizes that fulfillment of purpose is the reason for existence of all life. And, all of these, purpose works in harmony to bring about the universal purpose of sustaining life.

All beings living in the purpose that is to be fulfilled understands that one's purpose is akin to a goal one wishes to accomplish in life. For example, some may have a sole purpose of being parents while others may be teachers or engineers and so forth. The being will identify and be guided towards the purpose to be fulfilled through a strong attraction from the heart. The guiding attraction one experiences is a desire or pull towards one life path or another that will bring about the successful achievement of the being's ultimate objective to become a powerful creator with fulfillment of that individual's purpose. The attraction between the heart and what the heart desires allows the being to set up alignments and synchronicities that will act to work and manifest that individual's purpose into the physical three-dimensional reality for all of life's benefit.

All life forms have the potential to become powerful creators. Potential is absolutely a hidden skill that can be manifested if developed properly. Because the course of development differs greatly from individual to individual, there are a multitude of possibilities of potentials that may manifest from one conceptualized thought. One conceptualized thought can be shared between multiple individuals through each of those individuals' higher consciousness. This phenomenon is also known as singularity. It's the idea of a single material and in this case, that material is thought. Thought is the material that is shared with different individuals to be experienced in each of those individual's paradigms and is then to be actualized through each of those individual's respective realities.

The discovery and realization of purpose is one of the most important processes the human being must experience. It is this reason alone that all life exists - to become a powerful partner in the process of creation. The human being, specifically, must work to evolve the paradigm of life that is currently experienced into one that is more in harmonious with that of the universe. The coherence of the universe is due to the echo of frequency which is the vibratory speed of the cellular structure of that universe and its resonances determine the evolution of the universe and its constituents. The realization of purpose will require each human being to evolve into a higher vibratory individual with the capacity to embody the necessary connections to the higher conscious self. This connection, once maintained, is accomplished by the 5D+ being and allows for a continuous connection of the soul aspect of the self to the physical aspect of self, but only under certain biological and physiological conditions.

The biological and physiological conditions experienced by the human being during the evolutionary process of becoming a powerful creator assist the being in realizing and fulfilling that individual's purpose. The internal workings that the human beings undergo during the evolutionary process contribute to the being's expanded awareness of self. As the human being evolves, the awareness one experiences widens to that of the universal consciousness and the creative source. The being also understands through conceptualism that it is this universal consciousness that is responsible for the actions that lead to alignments and synchronicities in the physical reality. A being that reaches this point in the evolutionary processes realizes that physical reality can be manipulated and that manifestations can also be coordinated through the organization of alignments and synchronicities. It is the manipulation and recognition of alignment and synchronicities that lead to the production of that which was desired by the being's heart to best bring about one's fulfillment of purpose. The being has now begun to live in the purpose of fulfilling the heart's desire to become a powerful creator.

We can concluded, from this knowledge thaat we are all born with a divine destiny that is to be fulfilled in one of our spiritual lifetimes. The lifetime was chosen by you in your akash before your conception into the 3-dimensional physical reality. At a designated time in your existence alignments will occur that will bring about your ability to align yourself with the necessary synchronicities to manifest your purpose. Those alignments are created by the being's freedom of choice, the choice is to do the necessary work that was planned in your akash to bring forth the manifestations of your purpose in the 3-dimensional reality at a previously chosen time.

Once the being begins to work to align themselves with their destiny the necessary synchronicities begin to occur thus allowing for the successful accomplishment of bringing forth the vision that was communicated to you by your higher conscious. Once you are on track with your purpose the act of manifestation becomes almost automated as the you begin to create a consistent connection to the higher self the entanglement of soul and self as exhibited in the 5D+ being become one and you exist in a state of constant meditation continuously receiving and interpreting conceptual thought that brings forth your power to create.

ABOUT THE AUTHOR

Ler'e "Hustle God" Garrett, is an awakened being from the San Francisco bay area. Born and raised in her current hometown of Oakland, CA. Ler'e who goes by the alias "Hustle God", is a mother of 2 young men she raised as a single mother all while attending college and working 3 jobs. In college she received 4 college degrees, a Bachelor of Science in physical therapy with Cum Laude status, an associates degree in social and behavioral science, liberal arts and radiologic science. It was the combination of overcoming the struggles of her childhood, educational studies, a traumatic near-death experience and her spirituality that led up to the awakening that brought forth the knowledge that led to the development of *Become A Powerful Creator* the book and the motivational speaking series.

Made in the USA
Columbia, SC
19 January 2021

31207153R00057